A · TIME
TO · BE
BORN

A TIME TO BE BORN

JULIE MARTIN

THOMAS NELSON PUBLISHERS
Nashville

Published in Nashville, Tennessee, by Thomas Nelson, Inc., and distributed in Canada by Lawson Falle, Ltd., Cambridge, Ontario.

Unless otherwise noted, Scripture quotations are from the NEW INTERNATIONAL VERSION of the Bible. Copyright © 1978, New York International Bible Society.

Scripture quotations marked NKJV are from the New King James Version of the Bible. Copyright © 1979, 1980, 1982, Thomas Nelson, Inc., Publishers.

Library of Congress Cataloging-in-Publication information

Martin, Julie, 1963–
    A time to be born / Julie Martin.
        p. cm.
    ISBN 0-8407-7443-5
    1. Martin, Julie 1963—Health.   2. Miscarriage—Patients—United States—Biography.   3. Pregnant women—United States—Biography.
    I. Title
RG648.M36   1990
155.9′37—dc20
[B]   90–32672
                                                                    CIP

Printed in the United States of America
1 2 3 4 5 6 7 — 95 94 93 92 91 90

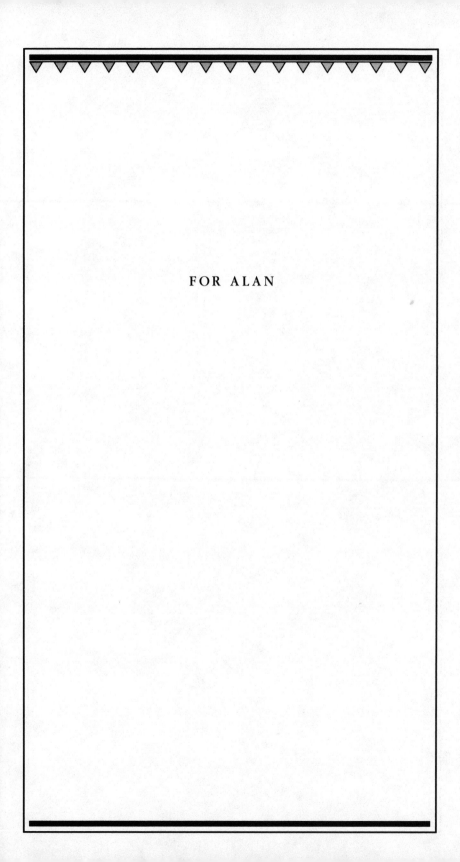

FOR ALAN

A SPECIAL THANKS

To Dr. Stephen Walker, who, with warmth and humor, brings hundreds of babies into the world each year.

To Bill Watkins and the other editors at Thomas Nelson for their input and encouragement.

To Julie "Spool" Meredith for helping secure permissions for this book.

To Ken Gire for teaching me so much about being a writer.

To Glenda Schlahta for taking time to review this book and offer her suggestions.

To Mom and Dad, Don and Jean Hedrick, for showing me what it means to trust God.

To Grandpa Herb and Grandma LaVonne Martin for Thursday afternoons.

To Rob and Linda Robertson for believing in this project and upholding me with prayer.

To Tom and Tambra Murphy for their constant support.

To Erica Lynn for her endless inspiration.

To everything there is a season,
A time for every purpose under heaven:
A time to be born,
And a time to die;
A time to plant,
And a time to pluck what is planted;
A time to kill,
And a time to heal;
A time to break down,
And a time to build up;
A time to weep,
And a time to laugh;
A time to mourn,
And a time to dance;
A time to cast away stones,
And a time to gather stones;
A time to embrace,
And a time to refrain from embracing;
A time to gain,
And a time to lose;
A time to keep,
And a time to throw away;
A time to tear,
And a time to sew;
A time to keep silence,
And a time to speak;
A time to love,
And a time to hate;
A time of war,
And a time of peace. . . .
He has made everything beautiful in its time.
Ecclesiastes 3:1–8, 11a (NKJV)

a
time
to
mourn

Conception.

Once a month spring visits a woman's body. Only during this four-day season can human life be planted, and only if the soil of her womb is prepared, and only then if the seed is implanted just so. When you ponder the precision conception requires, it's a wonder any of us are here at all.

Some call it a miracle.

The desire to have a child pounced on us like a puppy at play. One minute it was off in the corner licking at someone else's feet, and the next it was inextricably tangled in the shoestrings of our hearts.

Once the longing bit us, it had us mastered. Overnight, we began frequenting the church nursery, infant clothing departments, and children's book stores— just to look. And we actually started remembering the length and weight, pounds *and* ounces, of the babies born to our relatives and friends. The bursting world of parenthood was ripe for us, split wide open for us to taste. Now all we needed was a baby.

We can't finish our raisin bran. The stopwatch tells us we have two minutes to go—two minutes until we will race to the bathroom to read the results of the home pregnancy test. There on the tile counter of our makeshift lab, dunked in the last of a set of three vials, is a little plastic stick. If the stick is white, no baby this month. If it's blue, in nine months we will be parents. Never before has a simple strip of plastic been given so weighty a responsibility.

So we wait.

The two minutes drag their feet. They tease. They must know how anxious we are, yet still they amble—*tick, tick, tick*.

Finally, the watch beeps. And our hearts pound. We jump up from the kitchen table but then move slowly toward the bathroom.

Though the time is finally here, we don't hurry. There is something about this moment that makes us approach the room cautiously, even reverently. It seems a holy, fearful place, a place where we will discover a piece of God's plan for us. The time is here, our anxiousness gone. We have become like Moses, who, when he encountered God in the burning bush, stopped to remove his sandals.

"I can't look," I tell my husband.

"Come on, we have to," he answers with an eager smile.

Still in the hallway, we both peek through the bathroom door at the counter, and through the vial we see the little plastic stick—wearing deep-sea blue.

The waiting is over.

The miracle has begun. Life is budding in the enclosed garden of my womb.

i've been waiting for you
now no more wondering about me—
whether or not this miracle of life
would ever happen inside me

now i can wonder about you—
about what color threads
He's weaving you with

brown eyes or blue
will you like to swim or draw
*   bake bread or engineer buildings*
will you throw your head back and laugh hard
*   or just grin*
will you melt me with your daddy's smile

i don't know
i don't know

but i do know that i will love to hear you
*   call my name*
i will love to feel your tiny hand in mine
i will love to watch your tummy
*   rise and fall*
*   in sweet sleep*

and i know that sometimes you will
        hate me
sometimes you will shrink from my touch
sometimes your fevered breathing will
        rattle my soul
        in the dark
        dark night

but until then
please baby grow strong
take all you can from me
        please

until then
i'll be waiting for you

They say a mother has the keenest ear, that even while she sleeps, she hears. While one ear cushions itself in the pillow of the subconscious, the other guards the night air, listening for the most silent of sounds—a whimper, a wheeze, the rustle of crib sheets, the shuffle of pajamaed feet.

Exactly when this uncanny connection between a mother and her child is made, I don't know. I only know that during those early months, something deep inside me didn't feel right about the baby in my womb. I can remember several times lying on the couch in the evening, telling my husband, "I don't think our baby's alive." And he would reassure me that I didn't need to worry, that everything was fine.

I never quite accepted his words of comfort. I tried to believe I was just paranoid, like most expectant mothers who haven't yet heard a heartbeat or felt that first flutter in the womb, but I couldn't. When I strained to hear life's tiny, unformed voice, I heard nothing.

April 20, 9:00 A.M. Doctor's office.

There's no way we could forget my appointment today. It is my birthday, and what a birthday it will be. Today we will hear the baby's heartbeat. A friend has told us, "When you hear that sound, you'll fall in love."

The nurse seats us in one of the small, sterile rooms, and we wait, talking in hushed, sanitary tones.

Soon the doorknob clicks and turns, and we see the doctor's face in the doorway.

"Good morning," he says. "Let's see, you're in your fifteenth week? We oughta be able to hear that heartbeat today."

He pulls the doppler out of his white pocket and rolls it slowly across my bare stomach. We have been told that the baby's heartbeat will sound like a rhythmic whir, a *whoosh, whoosh, whoosh*. I am deaf to everything but my dream of hearing that sound.

After a minute of hearing only the pulse of my heart, the doctor assures us, "Sometimes the baby is in an awkward position, and we just can't pick up the heartbeat. Let's give it a little longer."

So the doppler continues its search. And we continue to hear the sound of my heart alone—and the pulsing silence. Another minute passes. Another eternal minute. The doctor slides the doppler back inside his coat.

"Things don't look good. We'd better do a quick ultrasound to see what's going on."

His words chill me. It's a doctor's job to reassure his patients, to put their fears to rest, right? He's supposed to tell me I've been worried for nothing. He's supposed to tell me everything's fine. But the hesitant concern in his voice and the flush of his face tell me our dream is about to turn into a nightmare.

Holding my husband's hand, I drag myself down the hall to the ultrasound room, lie down on the cold vinyl table, and wait in icy silence.

The doctor flips on the equipment and rolls the handpiece over my stomach, while I crane my neck for a view of the screen behind me.

At fifteen weeks, we should be seeing a fully developed baby exercising his limbs, heart rapidly pulsing. But focused on the screen is the blurred image of our baby, the size of a nine-week-old fetus, lifeless and still.

Hot tears numb my eyes. Time freezes. Frenzied thoughts gush through my mind in a torrent. I reach up from the table where I lie, pulling my husband close, and I bury my face in his chest.

"I'm sorry," the doctor says, hanging his head. "Sometimes the fetus just stops developing, and the mother fails to miscarry. I'm so sorry. I'd love to see you with a baby in your arms."

A missed abortion, they call it. A D&C is scheduled for this evening.

Until the surgery, I am to have nothing to eat or drink. Tonight, my birthday feast will be the drip of an IV and a few dry gulps of unconsciousness. Until then, I will go home and wait.

Loss and possession, death and life are one,
There falls no shadow where there shines no sun.[1]

1. Hillaire Belloc, "On a Sundial," *Sonnets and Verse* (London: Morrison and Gibb Ltd. 1923), 177.

As we round the last corner home from the doctor's office, our street seems more narrow. The house seems smaller, its paint more dull. It's as if my world has literally shrunk.

I want to run in the house and hide. But the first thing I see when my husband opens the front door is the phone.

"I guess I'd better call my parents," I tell him through a blanket of tears.

"Do you want to, or do you want me to?" he asks.

"No, I'll do it."

I would give anything if this pain could be ours alone. There's something hideous about knowing that a piece of news is going to devastate the hearts of those you love—makes you feel as though your tongue is a knife. I had been told the tragic news about our baby. The pain would never again feel as fresh to me. Yet I feared that hearing myself say the words "Mom, something awful. . . . The baby died" would make me feel afresh the stabbing, see again the still image on the black and white screen.

My mom is probably fixing lunch, pouring my dad a tall glass of milk, and I'm going to call and tell them that the baby I've been carrying, their grandchild, is dead? How can I disappoint them so? My older sister is pregnant too, and due just seven weeks before me. The babies were supposed to grow up and be best friends. Everyone was expecting to adore the little cousins—it was the talk all around the church we both attended.

I sit down on a hardbacked chair, pick up the phone, and shaking, I dial.

There are still seven hours until the surgery. Until then, I can't really mourn. I'm still carrying a child—not a life, but a child. Until then, I have to get something done. We have been scraping paint from the inside of our living room windows that weekend. The dull razor blades still lie on the table, where we had left them until another lull in our busy schedules allowed us to finish the job. We both change our clothes, and without discussing what to do next, pick up blades and start scraping.

Some would say scraping the paint off windowpanes at a time like this is unhealthy, running away, repressing the pain. But productivity is our novocain. A numbness sent from God. There will be time to be still and grieve, to hold each other and weep for our baby—and do nothing else. But for now, I just have to get something done.

As we work, the reality of our baby's death flickers on my mind's screen like the strobed flash of a home movie at the end of the reel. I can forget it in the calming darkness, but the glaring light of remembering makes my heart wince.

That sliver of paint in the corner, I'll get it if it's the last thing I. . . . Knuckles are in the way; I can't reach it. Can't reach it.

I've got to reach it.

The clank of the mailbox lid, the click of the mailman's heels on the white cement porch, tell me the mail is here. My husband opens the door and brings it in: the Pennysaver, a coupon for dish soap, the electric bill, a sweepstakes giveaway.

I hate the mail.

It stings like salt in my open wound.

It tells me that to everyone else, today is just another ordinary day.

The surgery takes place at the same hospital where the baby would have been born; I wear the same drab green gown I would have worn in labor and delivery. So many similarities between this death and the would-have-been birth of our baby. Yet so many differences.

it should've been october
when they wheeled me down the long hall and
into the room
hooked me up to an IV bag an EKG monitor a
blood pressure gauge
poked and probed and prepped
but at six months early
there are no videos of a baby screaming into life
in full color
just a black and white sonogram snapshot of a
baby still cradled in its tomb
no soft flesh to pass through me into life
just a sterile metal rod to scrape the death
from my womb
no certificate of birth
just a bottle of pills for the cramps
i guess that's what happens when it's only april
and
it should've been october

I want another dose of anesthesia, big enough to knock me out until the hurt is gone. I want to crawl back into that deep, black hole and hide.

Yet I know the pain will linger as long as I am numb. A preying lion, it will wait for me to wake up, and then pounce.

In order to heal, I must be willing to look my loss in the eyes. I have to be willing to accept that I've lost not just a mass of tissue or a dream of motherhood, but my baby.

Recovery room. Half an hour after the D&C.

The room is as cold as pain. Every tendon is a frozen cable, tensed and trembling against the bed.

"Why am I shaking?" I ask the nurse through clattering jaws.

"Honey, that's typical in recovery. Your body's trying to throw off the anesthesia. It should stop in about fifteen minutes."

What about this heartache? Can I throw it off too? If I shake long and hard enough, will it end?

Finally, the shaking stops. My body relaxes. The room seems warmer now. With a nurse gripping each elbow, I hoist myself off the bed and shuffle out the door.

But the next part of recovery will take some time.

He heals the brokenhearted
and binds up their wounds.
Psalm 147:3

You were dead six weeks before I ever knew. For six weeks I was your living casket.

There was nothing I could have done to help you. A mother relies on her child to communicate his pain. She looks and listens for the telltale signs: a cry, a hot forehead, bumps and rashes and bruises. But a child in the womb isn't seen, isn't heard. He must die alone.

I'll never even know whether you felt any pain.

April is the cruellest month, breeding
Lilacs out of the dead land, mixing
Memory and desire, stirring
Dull roots with spring rain.[2]

April is cruel because she is paradox.

Within her, barrenness and fertility are fused; death and life; futility and hope.

My mind goes back to another April 20, another year. 1983, the year of my mother's hysterectomy.

I visited her in the hospital that night, fascinated by the idea that I would be with her in the hospital on my birthday. Never had I been so close to what she actually experienced the day I was born. At the same time, I was filled with a sense of responsibility. Her operation was, in a way, a death. Gone was the possibility for her to have another child.

2. T. S. Eliot, "The Wasteland," *The Wasteland and Other Poems* (New York: Harcourt Brace Jovanovich, Inc., 1934), 29.

Tonight I saw you lying alone
  in a room of cold
    and colorless
    and clean
and I knew bright lights, blood,
  a fighting heartbeat, the stench of anesthetic

Twenty years ago
I filled your womb
  that sacred temple of life
You must've had dreams
  then
  for me

Now your womb lies barren
  a crypt
I only hope I have lived out some of those dreams
  you must have had
    for me
    then

And the best gift of all
is to see so purely
the life that you gave
the pain it was given in
Sleep mother
Sleep

Like my mother, on my birthday I, too, came to know the sterile room, the antiseptic smells. And in the hospital that night, I, too, came to understand that umbilically linked to every bunch of birthday balloons, every chocolate ice cream cake, is the dull throb of death.

When emotional shock first begins to wear off, your heart feels like a limb waking up from anesthesia: first it tingles, semi-consciously; then, as reality starts to seep in, it stings; and finally it fully wakes to the wrenching ache you will come to know better than your best friend.

The first few days after we found out about our baby were the easiest. Our hearts were soft, thankful. God's sovereign and loving control in our lives swept through our minds like cool water. We had been burned by loss, but He flooded us with grace.

He sent people to us to wrap us in their love and concern. And we let them. Friends brought baskets of flowers, cards, warm food. People we hardly knew grieved with us. Some shared that they, too, had lost a child. My husband and I drew close to each other. And, together, we clung to God.

Looking back, those few days at home with my husband seem like a dream. It was as though life stood still while we held each other and cried. But after a few days I went back to work, back to the routine of real life. Going back to work was like a sting that rouses you when you're dead asleep. It told me sharply, *Wake up, this is real*.

I climbed the stairs to my office, as I'd always done. I attended meetings, as I'd always done. I answered the phone, as I'd always done. But carrying the routine load of everyday life only reminded me that my arms were empty.

Yes, that's when the real pain begins. When everything in your life is back to normal except the one thing you've lost and are longing for. That's when you ache like a throbbing limb that's no longer numb. That's when you're fully awake.

i think the worst part of it all
is remembering us lying in bed
that morning
you held me close and sang
happy birthday to you happy
birthday to you happy
birthday dear julie happy
birthday
to you

I walk into the kitchen early this quiet morning, and with a twist of two fingers on the cold plastic rod, I open up the blinds. The wood floor creaks gently as I make my way to the table to set out the placemats for breakfast. As I reach to open the cupboard, something catches my eye. Resting in a ceramic bowl on the table is the opaque vitamin container marked *Prenatal*. I pick it up; it's heavy. I shake it, listening to the tablets rattle against the bottle's plastic sides. I read the label on the back. "A vitamin and mineral dietary supplement for use in prenatal care and lactation. Phosphorus Free." Clutching the vitamins, I drag a kitchen chair over to a high cupboard, open the door, and, straining to reach, set the container on the top shelf. I close the cupboard door and move the chair back to its place at the table. And, with spoons, knives, glasses, cereal bowls and paper napkins, I set the table for breakfast.

for my husband

i'm sorry
i know how much you wanted this baby
and i know you must be scared
> *wondering why something that seems to be*
> *so easy*
>> *for everyone else*
can be so difficult
>> *for me*
i want so badly to give you a child
you deserve to have your dream fulfilled
you are so good
> *and kind*
> *and filled with so much love to share*
i tried
> *and i failed*
i failed
and i'm so sorry

They say it's good for one who has lost a loved one to peer into the casket, even just briefly. The casket lies open to help the living close the lid on their relationship with the one who died, to help them accept with their hearts what they know in their minds—that the life in their loved one is gone.

With an early miscarriage there is no funeral, no viewing, no visual aid to bring closure to the heart.

We know nothing about our baby. We have no memories to help us mourn. There's nothing to let go of because there was nothing to hold on to, except a dream. There were no features that we had fallen in love with, no fingers that tapered like his dad's, no smile like his grandma's. No endearing ways about him, all his own. No laugh to ring in our minds when we think of him. Not even a memory of hearing his heart flutter through the doppler; he died too young.

We don't know anything about him, except that he was loved.

My frame was not hidden from you,
  When I was made in the secret place. . . .
Your eyes saw my unformed body.
All the days ordained for me
  were written in your book
  before one of them cause to be.

Psalm 139:15a, 16

It helps to believe that there was something wrong with you, that you just weren't developing properly and never would have been whole. I'm comforted when I think that I might have given you birth, kissed your damp head, only to watch death claim you slowly through the clear plastic walls of an incubator, or that you might have lived without arms and legs or the ability to think and feel. Then I can believe that God spared us all from a pain greater than that of losing you now. Only then.

But what if you would have been beautiful, bouncing with health? What, then, was the purpose in your dying? To teach us a lesson? To smooth a rough edge in our lives? Right now, I can see no grace in that.

It's not fair to you to hope you wouldn't have been healthy. But it's the only way I can justify losing you. It's the only way I can see God as merciful. It's the only way it wouldn't be my fault. I guess I need something to blame.

Please say something.

Don't just walk into my office, face like a blank sheet of paper, and proceed to hand me the work, business-as-usual. Something has happened to me. I am not the same person I was when I left the office last week. I have lost my baby, and it's killing me.

When you act like nothing has happened, it makes me feel that I should too. It says that you think losing a baby is either no big deal at all or so horrible it shouldn't even be mentioned. Either way, nothing feels more lonely.

Don't be afraid of saying the wrong thing. I'm not sure there is a wrong thing to say at a time like this. Even a blunder would feel better than this screaming silence. And, if you're really that concerned about saying the wrong thing, you could always just hug me. But whatever you do, don't just do nothing.

Please, somehow, acknowledge my pain.

It's amazing how quickly an expectant mother begins living for two. The moment she hears she's carrying a baby, her motivation for everything changes. Everything she eats, drinks, and breathes is sieved through the cheesecloth question: Is this good for the baby? She avoids eating sugar, taking medication, drinking anything containing Nutrasweet or caffeine. She eats more beef, drinks more milk, gets more sleep. She even lies down in the evening with her feet up.

I was no exception.

I gripped the handrail extra tight when I climbed down the stairway, so I wouldn't fall and hurt the baby. And I stopped by the drinking fountain an extra four or five times a day, for the baby. The way I sat, the way I ate, the way I went home right at 4:30—everything I did was for the baby.

It's hard to turn off this maternal mentality. It's been several weeks, but I still pause at the top of stairs to remind myself to be careful.

The bill came in the mail today. I didn't recognize the doctor's name on the return address. But when I opened the envelope and read the description of services, I remembered that we had met. "April 20, 1987. Anesthesia. D&C."

I shuddered. Had I really expected him to do it for free?

It was just a job, to him. Tidying up the death that had ravaged my dreams. At the end of the evening, he would go home to his family and forget the details of his day. Did I really expect him to weep for me?

Mother's Day came just two weeks after the D&C. The shock had worn off, and I was angry. At everything and everybody. The last thing I wanted to do was sit in church surrounded by mothers, beaming and wearing their perfumed corsages. And the thought of having to sit through a sermon on the value of motherhood made me sick to my stomach. It seemed to me that this day was being celebrated solely to rub my face in the fact that a mother I was not.

We spent the afternoon visiting my mother and then my mother-in-law. And I spent it angry at myself for being so saturated with grief that I wasn't able to honor our mothers in my heart. Being with our families made me angry. And hopeless about ever being a mother. But God used a stranger, an angel, to bring back my hope.

We left my family's home and stopped to eat at a place we had never been before. Hearing our footsteps, seeing the light flooding in through the door, smiling she met us at the hostess desk with an orchid and asked, "Are you a mother?"

I smiled politely and answered no.

"Then, are you expecting?" I shot a glance at my husband, swallowed hard, and again answered no.

"Well, then. You will be soon," she said so sweetly, and carefully pinned the flower to my dress.

There was something about the tone in her voice, the light on her face, the gentleness of her touch that I can't explain, but will never forget.

God used a woman I had never met to soften my hostility. That angry Mother's Day, it was hope she had pinned to my heart.

Blessed are those who mourn;
for they will be comforted.
Matthew 5:4

[41]

One warm afternoon at work, on my way out the door for a break, I passed by the desk of a woman I hadn't seen in several months. We rarely exchanged words when our paths crossed, but today she was going out of her way to be friendly.

As she heard me round the corner, she glanced up from her work, gave me a quick look-over, and then smiled. "You don't look very big."

I felt like a boulder had just rolled over my heart.

Still on my way out the door, I stopped cold in my tracks, took a deep breath, and answered, "I'm sorry—you didn't hear? I lost the baby about a month ago." Her face turned white, and she mumbled a quick apology and turned again to her work.

I have a feeling she hurt worse than I did that afternoon. But I'll never know. She never spoke to me again.

I forgave her. And I hope that soon after I left her that afternoon she forgave herself.

She didn't know.

God, I am ashamed.

Ashamed because I feel that throbbing every time I hear that so-and-so is pregnant, or just had her baby—especially if the baby wasn't planned. I want to be happy for them. But my own yearning keeps getting in the way.

And so I sin, Lord. By wanting what they have, now. By choosing not to believe that you know what's best for our family. And that life is in your hands.

Though the fig tree does not bud
*   and there are no grapes on the vines,*
though the olive crop fails
*   and the fields produce no food,*
though there are no sheep in the pen
*   and no cattle in the stalls,*
yet I will rejoice in the LORD,
*   I will be joyful in God my Savior.*
The Sovereign LORD is my strength;
*   he makes my feet like the feet of a deer,*
*   he enables me to go on the heights.*
                                    Habbakuk 3:17–19

For many women who miscarry, getting pregnant again is the farthest thing from their minds. Some are afraid of losing another baby, a pain that at the time seems unbearable. Others just need time to grieve the past without the distraction of planning for the future. And others have silent reasons of their own.

But for me, conceiving again would be part of the healing. Part of the pain of losing our baby was that I so yearned for a child. Nausea, fatigue, toxemia—I would gladly take it all for the chance to carry another child. And the sooner God chose to fill that longing, the better.

HANNAH'S PRAYER

(see 1 Samuel 1:1–18)

Hannah, you knew longing like you knew your own
   heartbeat
Year after year your arms were empty
And Peninnah's were full
While you poured out your kneeling soul to the
   Lord
  the sounds of her children skipping, singing—the
  bubbling laughter—just outside your window
  must have made a lump rise
   in your throat
And that she, grinning, had sent them to play near
   your room
  must have made coals burn in your eyes
You fasted
   You wept
     You grieved
You pleaded with God to give you a child
Every month was a mourning, and yet you waited
   still

That was all you could do

a

time

to

plant

Maybe the wind was too strong. Maybe the bud, too weak. Maybe next time the season of my womb will be fairer.

Next time. Three months later.

I think I might be pregnant. It's unbelievable, I know. Yet, this moodiness, this sluggishness; and food sounds horrible. But it just can't be. That would be too gracious of. . . . Please God, don't tease me.

The next morning we bring out the home test again, dunk the little plastic stick, and wait. But the waiting is different this time. I don't care if it takes forever. I have convinced myself I'm not pregnant, my thumb pressed firmly on disappointment's head. We are doing the pregnancy test just to rule out the possibility, right, honey? I probably just have the flu.

While the stopwatch ticks the time away, we make bread-and-butter conversation, keeping all emotion safely on the shelf.

But the time comes quickly. Time to check the color of the little plastic stick. Time, we have convinced ourselves, to see that it's exactly as we expected, all white, not a trace of blue.

We walk into the bathroom together, and there on the counter, swimming in the last of the vials, is a little blue stick.

Cool tears.

And hugs.

And thanks to our God.

Hope deferred makes the heart sick,
*   but a longing fulfilled is a tree of life.*
Proverbs 13:12

you have heard me God
you saved my tears in your wineskin
 till the salty sting was gone
you purified them with grace and made them
 a sweet spring rain
that you have lavishly poured on me to water
 my dusty heart
so what can i do for you
who can i be for you
how can i bloom for you
because you have heard me my God

I am thankful, yes. But more nauseated than the flu bug itself.

Food in the stomach is so . . . temporary. A box of saltines waits in every room. The bed is full of crumbs from the peanut butter toast I ate at 3:00 A.M. Brushing my teeth takes all morning. And the smell of his soap makes me keep my freshly showered husband at least twelve feet away.

Not only is my appetite temperamental, but also my feelings. Every emotional nerve is raw and exposed, and interprets my husband's most innocent comment as the chilly air of insult. And my moods dip and soar like a bat in the night.

I imagine most couples are humored by this prenatal pendulum. Who wouldn't be, knowing they only had to make it through a few rough months, and that at the end of it all their bouncing baby would be born?

Part of us was amused too—the tenacious optimism in us. "I'll be seeing you soon," I would say as I nibbled down my dinner. But another part, a large and beastly part, whispered in our ears that we might endure the vomiting, the fatigue, the mood swings, only to lose this baby too. That possibility sobered us. We kept it ever in the forefront of our minds.

Are you alive?

Will I ever hold you? Will I ever hear you call my name?

Please, little one, live.

The front door of the doctor's office swings slowly open on its tired hinge today. The waiting room is full. There is one seat next to a very pregnant woman flipping through the latest *Parent* magazine. I grab a copy of *People* and sit down.

After a few minutes, I notice her poking her huge stomach. Trying not to let her see me looking, but failing, I smile. "Is the baby kicking?"

"Yes. Hard! But I can't tell whether it's a foot or an elbow," she says, still poking.

"When are you due?"

"Last week." She rolls her eyes. "Are you pregnant?"

"Uh, yes. I am. Just nine weeks."

Just then the side door opens, and the assistant calls a name.

"That's me," she says, easing her way out of the chair. "Well, good luck with your pregnancy."

"Thanks. And I hope the baby comes soon." I watch her waddle through the door.

The doctor has been monitoring me carefully during these first few weeks of my pregnancy, and today, at nine weeks, he will do an ultrasound to check for the baby's heartbeat. An ultrasound can detect the movement of a baby's heart weeks before it can ever be heard.

"Julie?" The assistant pokes her head out the door and calls.

Taking a deep breath, I get up from my chair and walk toward the door.

Something in that breath of air makes me cringe. Just the smell of the room alone takes me back to that morning we found out our baby had died. The furniture, the carpet, the magazines—everything smells like bad news.

"Come on back," says the assistant. "How are you?" she adds warmly.

"Oh, fine, thanks," I reply as we make our way down

[53]

the hall. The memory of my last trip to this room floods my mind like warm liquid. This must be what it feels like to return to the scene of a heinous crime committed against someone you love.

I lie down on the vinyl table and wait for the technician to prepare the equipment.

"You're in your ninth week?" she asks.

"Yeah," I answer, staring at the Georgia O'Keefe print on the wall.

"Good. We should see the baby's heartbeat today."

She picks up the handpiece and rolls it over my bare stomach. Instantly, a fuzzy-gray picture appears on the screen.

"There's the baby," she says, pointing to a blurry white image the size of a kidney bean. "And look. See that movement? That's the heart."

That's the heart.

I see the heart.

I see life awake, a tiny heart leaping proudly as if to say, "Hello, yes, I'm here and I'm growing strong. Please, really, you can love me now."

"Everything looks good," the technician says.

Yes. Everything looks good.

I get dressed quickly, stop by the desk to set up my next appointment, and walk through the crowded waiting room to the door. On my way out, I catch the eye of a young woman with a huge stomach. And I smile.

The remaining seven months stretch before me like a desert. I realize that a heartbeat at nine weeks doesn't guarantee anything. We could still lose the baby.

But I have a decision to make. Will I open my heart and love this child—not in a few months or once he's born—but now? Or will I keep my heart slammed shut in fear? Do I dare risk being hurt again by letting myself form a bond with this unborn baby?

It would be easier to lock my heart's door and throw away the key till I have proof I will see this child. Yet I can't help but think that a baby somehow senses the love of his parents even while in the womb. It wouldn't be fair to the baby to starve him of this early love. There's a budding life inside me; I've got to let myself be excited about it. If life begins at conception, then so must my love.

The phone rang only once before she picked it up.

"Hi, Mom." I greeted her warmly.

"Julie?" She answered abruptly. "Is everything okay?"

I had called at an odd hour. An hour when a phone call usually means either a wrong number or tragic news. To her, hearing my voice on the phone so early in the morning could only mean bad news.

"Yeah, Mom, everything's fine. I was just wondering if . . ."

She didn't hear me. She was so relieved I wasn't calling about the baby that it didn't matter what else I told her. I shouldn't have called, not so early. Not when I was bound to frighten her.

I wish I could erase it. I wish I could just blot out the fact that I lost my first baby, and start over. But I can't. It will always be part of the story of my life. Breezing my way through pregnancy will forever be out of my reach.

So everybody is watching me. And I don't blame them. Lightning can strike twice in the same place. They need to be careful to protect themselves from hurt. With everything I've got, I must try to share with them the calm He has placed in my heart.

Trust in the LORD forever,
for the LORD, the LORD, is the Rock eternal.
Isaiah 26:4

September, 9:00 A.M. Doctor's office.

Today is the day we will hear the baby's heartbeat. I remember again my friend's words: "When you hear that sound, you'll fall in love."

The nurse seats us in the first room on the right and tells us it'll be just a few minutes. So we wait, joking about the paper-napkin robe I have to wear.

Soon the doorknob clicks and turns, and we see the doctor's face in the doorway.

"Good morning," he says. "You're at the end of your twelfth week? Let's find that heartbeat."

He rolls the doppler across my bare stomach.

Instantly we hear it.

Instantly, the *whoosh, whoosh, whoosh*.

My husband takes a step closer to the table and touches my hand.

The doctor rolls the doppler to the other side of my stomach; the heartbeat grows fainter.

"The baby's chest must be over here," he explains, moving the instrument back to where we had heard the prancing whir. "You can hear it strongest when the doppler's right over the heart."

"It's beating so fast," I say.

"It's working hard. In a couple of months, it'll sound like a gallop, and we'll have to turn the speaker down," the doctor answers dryly.

"Well, looks great," he tells us, sliding the doppler back into his pocket. "Do you guys have any questions?"

My husband and I look at each other; I see the dance in his eyes.

We shake our heads and answer, "No. No questions."

Morning sickness.

Quite the understatement. It usually lasts all day. How ironic to spend the first part of pregnancy, this most romantic, expectant period of life, with my head in the toilet. Since pregnancy is the symbol of fertility, life, and health, sickness should be its foil. For at least three months, pregnancy and nausea are linked at the belly.

My adult mind still likes to ask the toddler question, *Why?*

Maybe God sends us morning sickness to initiate us into motherhood—an act of grace delivered tongue-in-cheek. After three months of nausea, the trauma of midnight feedings, teething, and occasional ear infections can hardly daunt the toughened-up mom. Or maybe it's for a more practical reason. To get us to slow down.

Nausea and fatigue, those stubborn prenatal nurses, force an expectant mother to take care of herself by making fast-paced living nearly impossible. Enormous metabolic and hormonal changes in the pregnant woman send her system reeling. The hungry microscopic cluster of cells—every minute dividing and multiplying to form life—burns sleep and guzzles vitamins, minerals, and proteins from the mother's body. Every extra minute of sleep, every milligram of minerals is richer soil for the budding life. And so she rests. And sleeps. She has no choice.

This putting-on-the-brakes gives us time not only to rest our bodies, but to humbly lay down our spirits on God's altar for the awesome task ahead. In just a few months, He will entrust us with a child. And we will be to that child what our parents were to us—the symbol of God, the very force of life and lasting love.

Glowing? Energetic? Maybe later. For now, I am as pale as a soda cracker. And humble as pie.

I don't even remember where I was. But it doesn't matter. For, suddenly, while I was there, I felt it. The quickening. The first time I felt you move inside me.

It felt to me like a butterfly kiss, like the brushing of eyelashes across my bare cheek.

And it meant that you are incredibly alive, and big enough now to nudge me with a hand or foot or elbow when you stretch.

Big enough to make me stop everything, and for a moment forget where I am, and think of you.

Week sixteen. I sit in the waiting room with my husband, guzzling my third sixteen-ounce styrofoam cup of water.

In the sixteenth week of a pregnancy, my doctor routinely does an ultrasound to measure the baby's head and limbs so the estimated due date can be double-checked and any serious problems detected.

Ultrasounds are completely painless, except for one small torture. They are more effectively done when the patient has a full bladder. And not the kind of full bladder you can laugh about. The kind that makes you sweat.

The uterus is located behind the bladder, so a full bladder creates a window through which the fetus can be viewed. The fuller the bladder, the clearer the picture. And what mother wouldn't want the best possible picture of her baby?

"Julie?" The assistant calls through the door.

I smile politely as my husband helps me and my forty-eight ounces out of the chair. And I slosh down the hall.

The sonogram. We are about to snatch a glimpse of the miracle of life. Do we dare?

Lying on the cool vinyl table, I look over my shoulder at the black screen. The doctor flips on the switch. An image appears. A rough circle halved by a thin white line, each half cloistering a pearl.

"That's the top of the head," the doctor says, pointing to the gray image. "That line divides the two hemispheres of the brain, and those are the two brain lobes." Wait, we've never gotten this far before.

Suddenly, the head turns. With a twist of the baby's neck, what had looked like a textbook photo of a fetus's brain comes alive.

"See, there's an arm. And the other one."

Two thin limbs swim into the picture, the fluid arms of a skeleton marionette. The baby holds his hand still for a few seconds as if posing. Look at the tiny fingers. One, two, three, four, five. I squeeze my husband's hand.

The legs appear, knees bent, kicking gracefully. Then, as if the puppeteer had given the string a quick yank, the baby jerks its body around. Such rough movements! And all I've been feeling is an occasional brush on the inside of my womb.

"There's the spine," says the doctor. The string of vertebrae serpentines in and out of the picture as the baby twists its lithe body.

"You guys are going to have your hands full. Good thing it's your first."

The doctor rolls the handpiece to a new position. The image clears. There's a close-up of the baby's face. Two eye sockets, the nasal cavity, the mouth. The face, completely formed.

"See that round, bright structure?" the doctor says, pointing to the eye socket. "That's the eyeball."

The mouth begins to move. "And there. The baby's

drinking the amniotic fluid. We've even seen some at this age sucking their thumbs." I shoot my husband a smile.

And just beneath the head, the heart steadily claps in the baby's chest. I can see them. One, two, three, four. All four chambers of the heart.

Still the baby's limbs are moving, swaying in the currents that fuel the womb.

"There are all four paws," says the doctor, counting the hands and feet. "The thing in the center, that's the cord. His lifeline."'

There is a child within me. A life within a life. Sharing blood. Sharing food. Sharing breath.

The doctor measures the baby's head and then turns off the machine. "Everything looks great, and I'll see you next month." He's got to go. Another patient is waiting for him in the other room.

I get dressed quickly, hug my husband tightly. And I wonder if God allowed the angels to watch Him form Adam from the dust.

For you created my inmost being;
*   you knit me together in my mother's*
*   womb.*
I will praise you because I am fearfully and
*   wonderfully made. . . .*
                            Psalm 139:13, 14a

At sixteen weeks a fetus is fully formed. He is only six and three-fourths inches long, weighs only about five ounces. But he has eyebrows. He has fingernails and toenails. He can hear.

And he can be killed. Legally. Because a mother has decided it would be inconvenient to have a baby right now, or thinks she's too old, or isn't through high school yet and what would her parents think? After all, she's got her rights.

But what if she were made to watch her baby on a sonogram? What if she saw with her own eyes that this mass of tissue had a profile? What if she counted the fingers and toes and saw the tiny heart beating in his chest? Could she kill her baby then?

The morning was cool and bright. The kind of morning that makes you breathe consciously, just to take in your fill of the fresh air. I got to work early so I could be alone before the morning clatter distracted my heart. A bouquet of flowers and a redwood planter of pansies brought by friends decorated my desk. This day had been bathed in the prayers of those close to me. It was October 8, the due date of the baby we had lost.

I pulled out my chair, sat down comfortably, and brushed a hand across the small lump protruding from my stomach. Inside me was a life. God had mercifully given me the hope of bearing a child.

There I sat, carrying a baby, yet my womb was still aching for the loss of another. Never had I known mourning so mingled with grace. Loss and hope shared a seat in my heart, each keeping the other from complete overthrow. A time to mourn, and a time to dance—but today I would have both at once.

And the main thing that will keep the mourning from winning out today is knowing that the Lord Jesus was the first thing my baby ever saw.

october 8

you were born into heaven's arms
where every day is a celebration
> *of a life*
>> *that never ends*

one day we will join you at the Table
and you will tell us about your life with Jesus
> *about the gift of love He's given you*
> *that will never be broken or lost*

so although we will never scoot you up to our table
> *teach you how to blow out your candles*
> *wipe the frosting from your face*
> *or give you stuffed tokens*
> > *of our love*
today in our hearts we will sing with the angels
happy birthday to you, dear baby
happy birthday to you

The second trimester, when the womb begins to bulb, robs a pregnant woman of a very significant right. The right to her own stomach. At no other time in her life will mere acquaintances, men included, pat her stomach on a whim.

She is sharing her body with the baby, lending her womb to the child. And the whole world knows it. The whole world sees her stomach no longer as a part of her, but as a kind of prenatal bassinet that everyone has permission to poke and rub.

In fact, much of her private life goes public. Her diet, weight gain, and sleeping habits become common knowledge. Her body is not her own.

Does she mind?

Should she mind?

I don't think so.

If she loses her privacy in exchange for people's wonder at the miracle she carries, there is really no cost at all.

The room hums with conversation like a beehive. It is filled with people, alive with their movement and laughter. At this company-wide birthday celebration, I am mingling with a group of people when a girl in the circle asks, "How far along are you?"

"Just starting my seventh month," I answer.

Another woman, concerned, asks if the doctor is still watching me closely and if he says everything is okay with the baby. I confidently tell her that the doctor says the baby's doing beautifully.

But the puzzled look on the girl's face tells me she doesn't know I had miscarried.

"Did you know that I lost a baby a few months before this pregnancy?" I ask. I always hate to give the news. It feels like I'm soliciting sympathy. And I hate the way it's guaranteed to make heavy the conversation's tone.

"Oh . . . no. I didn't. How far along were you?"

"About four months. But the baby had stopped developing at about nine weeks." I like to tell people how early it happened so they won't worry about me anymore.

"Oh, how awful. You know, that happened to my sister-in-law. But she was in her seventh month. The baby seemed to be perfectly healthy, and then one day he just stopped moving. They think the cord wrapped around his neck and strangled him. But she got pregnant again right away, and her little girl is two now."

Just starting my seventh month. My own words echo in my head. So the baby's not safe yet. Not safe.

The conversation turns to other things. I excuse myself from the group, walk back to my office alone—and I pray.

And in that quiet room, God gives me a hard and tender reminder. The planting is His. The sowing is His. The child is a gift.

On the glass table by the couch rests a book about pregnancy and childbirth. Through sketches and photos, it charts the development of a fetus from fertilized egg to full-term infant. Almost every evening, I pick it up and skim the well-worn pages. I want to know all I can about the baby. The womb is closed to my eyes, but the book provides a paper-and-ink window through which the budding mystery can be partially viewed.

Through the pages of the book, I have watched the baby grow from what looked like a grain of rice, to a coffee bean, to a tadpole, to a human being with all his limbs and organs, yet small enough to nestle into a teacup. Touching my stomach, I have gazed at the pictures and tried to imagine the baby deep within my body to be just like the photograph.

Tonight, in my seventh month, the book shows the baby fully developed, filling the womb. His arms are bent at the elbows, folded across his chest, and his legs are frogged to his chin. But even with the drawing right in front of me, it doesn't seem possible that a whole, healthy baby, that big, is actually inside me. I can feel the movement, even watch an elbow or knee roll across my abdomen, but still a small part of me won't be convinced until the baby is born. A doubting Thomas, I must see.

With two months left till the due date, the room we called the "baby's room" was fit for anything but a baby. It was our laundry room, library, gift wrap center, and all-around spare closet.

The walls were dingy and peeling, pocked with old nail holes. The floor was spattered with paint and black scuff marks streaked deep into the wood grain. It was a mess. That our baby, pink and new, would ever sleep there seemed absurd. Transforming the room would require no less than the touch of Midas.

So we started in. Little by little, weekend by weekend, we gutted the room.

First, we found a new place for everything and threw out everything that didn't need a place. That left us with an empty room. Filthy, but empty.

Next, we washed down the walls, spackled them, and gave them a fresh coat of paint. It looked more like a nursery already.

Then, carpet. Something dark to hide the stains it would inevitably collect. Once the carpet was laid, my husband and I would often sit in the room in the evenings and talk, just us and the smells of anticipation—new carpet and fresh paint.

So far, it had been easy. Decisions had been minor; we hadn't yet dealt with the room's decor. But now we had to choose wallpaper and furniture for a baby whose sex and personality were a complete mystery. Should we choose bold colors or soft? A pattern whimsical or sober? Airplanes or dolls? We decided on an androgynous decor that could be feminized with a valance here, some eyelet there, should the baby be a girl.

It is finished now. Arm in arm, we stand at the door and peer in.

The nursery is clean, but empty. A garden, tilled, waiting for the first flower to bloom.

I can't sleep.

I open my eyes, and all I see are the clock's bold, red numbers glaring through the darkness: 2:43. My husband lies beside me, breathing quietly, still.

But I am not the only one awake; I have company. The baby has joined an intrauterine karate club and is practicing his kicks.

I roll from side to back so I can feel with both hands the tiny limbs and joints that jab the wall of my watermelon womb. Suddenly the baby packs a hardy punch and extends his foot or fist to full length. I push lightly on the joint. He retracts it. It appears again, fully extended, just a few inches lower. I push on it again. Again he retracts it, cat and mouse. Finally, I grab the joint between two fingers and gently squeeze. For a few seconds it is calm, caught. But then it escapes my grip and pokes through the thin skin a little higher. I roll back to my side, rest my stomach against my husband's sleeping back, and wait. Then another jab, a strong one. And he feels it, sure enough. "What was that?" he mumbles.

"It was the baby. We're both awake, and we didn't want you to miss out."

He rolls over and places his hand on my stomach without a word. Such a sport. Soon I hear his soft snore. And the baby has quit kicking; he must be asleep.

It's 3:08. The night is still again. The bold, red numbers of the clock fade to black as I close my eyes and watch the shades of sleep.

The table is set with the everyday dishes for two. The stove simmers with covered pots that spatter boiling water onto the warm stove top and make it sizzle. And I am tearing damp lettuce, dropping it into a salad bowl, when I hear the front door opening with a creak and then my husband's tired shoes scuffing cheerfully along the tile floor.

I walk to the door to greet him. He pulls me close with a smile and touches my full, round stomach. "Hi. How are the two of you?"

"Pretty good. A little tired," I answer.

"Well, when did you get home? You didn't work late, did you?" he asks with a crinkled brow.

"No. In fact, I came home early. I just can't concentrate. The baby must be using all my oxygen and leaving nothing for my brain."

He smiles and follows me back into the kitchen.

"How was your day?" I ask, stirring dinner.

"Oh, okay. It's good to be home."

"Remember, we said we would decide on a name for the baby tonight." I remind him.

"That's *right*. What have you been thinking?"

Pouring the milk, I give him my list of boy's names.

"Man," he says melodramatically. "I don't want my son to have one of those sissy names."

Amused at his bombastic response, I say, "But all the traditional boy's names are so common. Do you want five other kids with his name in his class? Hey, let's eat."

He loosens his tie and asks what we're having.

"Spaghetti, broccoli, and green salad."

As I serve up the steaming noodles, he tells me a tale about his day. "Poor girl, drove right through the arm of the gate and smashed into the security door. It was wild."

"How awful. Honey, what do you think, if the baby's a girl, about giving her a family name? All the pretty

[75]

family names are taken. So it seems like we have two choices. We can either pass down a family name or give her a name she'll like." I reach for the Parmesan cheese. "Did you hear about the plane that blew up off the coast? What happened?"

"They aren't sure, but they think it might have been a bomb," he answers, twirling spaghetti on his fork. Then he throws out a name. "How about that for a boy?"

"Yeah. I like it. But I can already hear the nicknames he'll get called."

The phone rings. He reaches over and picks it up. I put an elbow on the table and rest my chin in my hand.

"Hello?" A pause. "Mmm hmm. Uh . . . sorry, we're not interested. Bye." He hangs up. "Guess what. Out of three million people, we were selected to win a trip for two to the Bahamas."

"They always call at dinner. Hey, what do you think of this for a girl's middle name?"

He takes a drink of milk and then answers. "I wouldn't worry too much about the middle name. She'll only hear it when she's either graduating or in trouble."

"Want some more spaghetti?" I ask, reaching for the bowl of noodles.

"Sure. Sounds good." He serves himself another plate of pasta. "How about this for a boy?" he asks.

"Oh, we can't use that name. There was this strange kid in my fourth grade class who had that name."

"Did you get a chance to go to the post office today?" he asks, putting down his fork.

"Nope. Had a lunch meeting," I answer through a yawn. "Honey, let's go into the living room and finish talking. I'll do the dishes later."

In the living room, I flop on the couch, and my husband sits on the floor by my head.

"Is that plant dying?" he asks, looking at the wilting ficus in the corner of the room.

"Here. The name book is right here." I reach down and pick up the copy of *10,000 Baby Names* on the floor by the couch. I scan a few pages quickly and toss out a name.

"I can picture a baby girl with that name, but not a grown woman," he says, still staring at the plant.

"I'm getting sleepy, sweetheart," I say, and hand him the book. "What time do you have to leave in the morning?"

He flips through the pages of *Baby Names* and finds a good possibility. "What about this one?" he asks enthusiastically.

"Yeah. I like it," I mumble. "What does it mean?"

"It means . . . 'deceitful.' Yeah. Forget it."

He keeps searching for that perfect name, and the next time he asks my opinion he gets no answer. He slips out of the room and returns with a blanket. Covering me with it as I sleep, he bends to kiss my forehead. "We'll decide later," he whispers. Then he turns and quietly leaves the room.

I feel like a cow.

Yes, a cow. A big, brown speckled one. My swiftness has been replaced by a kind of grazing. I graze from place to place absentmindedly, eating my leafy vegetables, full of calcium and iron.

I cannot see my feet, but I know they are there. They are swollen from the heat and the weight of the stomach I carry.

I feel so like a cow.

Childbirth class.

We enter the room, pen, notebook, and pillows in hand, and sit down on two folding chairs in the corner. The room is already full of pregnant women and their coaches. In six two-hour sessions, we will all learn how to survive labor and delivery.

The first thing we learn are the two key words, words to wear like a motto on a badge, words, our instructor tells us, by which to live or die: *relax* and *concentrate*.

She explains that one of the keys to relaxing is regular, rhythmic breathing. At the beginning of labor, we should breathe slowly, steadily, and deeply. As the pain gets hotter and the eyes get wider, we will want our breaths to be shorter and closer together. "Okay, moms, lie down on your backs with your knees bent. Remember, your breaths are supposed to be slow and deep. Relax! Coaches, sit at Mom's left side, rub her shoulders and neck, and talk to her. Tell her to relax. Tell her to concentrate. Tell her she's doing great."

We all get up from our seats and make ourselves comfortable on the carpet. From my position on the floor, I raise my head and glance across the room. It looks like a field full of mole hills, each one guarded by a dubious mole.

For at least five minutes, we practice our slow-paced breathing and touch relaxation, and I endure several of my husband's most sincere "You're-doing-great-honey's" and "Relaaaax. Coooooooooon-centrate's" without laughing, before the instructor's welcome voice breaks in to teach us the next phase of our strategy.

"When labor gets a little rougher, we do what's called patterned breathing. The coach will call out a number or hold up his fingers to tell you how many times to breathe. You will breathe however many times he tells you, with your mouth shaped to say 'heeeee.' And then you'll finish with a breath shaped to say 'hooooo.' So if he holds up three fingers, you'll go 'heee, heee, heee, hooo' and then look for the next number. The rhythm and repetition will help calm the mom and also help take her mind off the contractions. Okay. Let's try it."

Still lumped on the floor, we moms lay our heads back and watch for the number. My coach holds up two fingers. "Heee, heee, hooo," I breathe.

"Oh, I forgot to tell you coaches not to hold up more than five fingers or your wife might hyperventilate," the instructor adds with a grin.

My next number is four. "Heee, heee, heee . . ." I can't finish without bursting into hysterical laughter. My husband-coach loses it too. The teacher sees us shaking in the corner, smiles, and gives us a pretend reprimand.

Next, we learn about focal points. "A focal point is an object on the wall or across the room that you can center on to distract you from the pain," the instructor tells us. A focal point can also be imaginary; it can be a mental image of yourself sunning on a sizzling tropical island, sipping a cold drink from a coconut. Whether your focal point is an old nail in the wall or a paradise, the principle is the same: concentrate on something else to take your mind off the pain.

Besides these techniques, we also learn every detail of what happens to both mother and baby during labor and delivery. By the end of the class, the terms *dilation, effacement, fundus, transition,* and *episiotomy* roll off our tongues like the ABCs.

We used to wonder why it was necessary to know everything about childbirth; women in other countries just go squat in a field when it's time to have their babies, and women have been having babies for centuries without so much as reading a pamphlet about it. Now we know why it's necessary to know. So we can be prepared.

We leave the room on the last night of class. The

notebook is full; we're prepared. We know all the "might happens" of labor and delivery. But even with all our knowledge, the hows and whats of this first baby's birth will be a mystery—until it happens.

A baby shower.

A celebration for the baby and me while we're waiting to meet.

I enter the room and take a sweeping look; everywhere I see care. The room dances with balloons. Food refreshes on one table, gifts shimmer on another. And it's all for me and the baby. Tonight, friends and family show they are waiting with me, helping the waiting to pass.

We share a laugh, many laughs. And a prayer for my baby. *Thank you, dear God, for this precious life, and please may delivery be smooth and completely painless.*

Then they tell me to open the gifts. There are so many boxes, bows, and ribbons tied with rattling toys. Yes, open them. Friends. Already loving my baby. Go ahead, open them.

So tiny, everything. A stuffed pink elephant. Bath towels with hoods. Receiving blankets spotted with clowns. Fuzzy booties. A book of rhymes. A footed sleeper. Size zero shoes. We pass them around the room so everyone can sigh and *ooh* and *ahh*.

It's getting late. Some have gone home. The stragglers help load the trunk with the balloons and the gifts.

I will take them all home to the baby's room. The tiny gifts will help fill the baby's closet and drawers. They will give me something to fold and hang while I wait.

Anticipation—
Sweet fulfillment just out of reach.
Friday morning, the whole weekend ahead.
The savory smell of a favorite meal cooking.
A red rose, petals closed.
Packing the honeymoon suitcase.
The last fifteen minutes before he's due home.
A nursery—full closet, empty crib.
Anticipation—
The cream skimmed off the top of experience.
We wait forever. Take our fill.
Then quickly forget the joy of longing.
Anticipation—
Waiting room for a dream-to-be.
I will stop and linger there.

HANNAH'S ANSWER

(see 1 Samuel 1:19, 20)

The months pass like years of winter
        each a throbbing echo of the one before
Until one day you notice that something is different
you touch your stomach and know that
        the chill is gone
you put your spirit's ear to the womb
        and hear Yes

Hannah, He remembered you
The cold waiting is done
Now you can long for your child
        as the winter waits for spring
Knowing it will come
Knowing the frozen branches have thawed
        and soon will bring fruit

a
time
to
dance

*"They will come and shout for joy on the
        heights of Zion;
they will rejoice in the bounty of the LORD—
the grain, the new wine and the oil,
        the young of the flocks and herds.
They will be like a well-watered garden,
        and they will sorrow no more.
Then maidens will dance and be glad,
        young men and old as well.
I will turn their mourning into gladness;
I will give them comfort and joy instead
        of sorrow.
I will satisfy the priests with abundance,
        and my people will be filled with
        my bounty,"* declares the Lord.

Jeremiah 31:12–14

They're known as Braxton Hicks contractions, only because the mother of the man who discovered the phenomenon, Mrs. Hicks, named her son Braxton.

These contractions feel like a thick, wide, rubber band being pulled taut across your womb and then slowly let go. You feel hot; your face gets flushed; your stomach feels basketball hard. The baby is still, hugged tight in the contracting womb.

Braxton Hicks contractions are a kind of rehearsal for labor. The problem is you can never be sure what they mean. Since they often begin in the second trimester, they may mean nothing at all; like a concert violinist, maybe the womb is just being diligent by practicing a little early. Or maybe it's rehearsing for the last time before the big concert, the birth, coming up in just an hour. All you can do is breathe through the contractions and keep track of how close together they are. If they keep coming harder and closer together, pack your bag. It just might be the real thing.

The church is warm and humid on this Sunday evening. The electric fan on the high ceiling frantically spins, doing its best to cool the sanctuary. I sit next to my husband in the pew. My Bible is open across what there is of my lap; my legs are crossed at my swollen ankles.

Then it grips me—a Braxton Hicks. The pastor's voice fades; the heat rolls through my body; it surges up through my face and hovers in my ears. A veritable heat wave.

"Are you okay?" my husband whispers, leaning his head toward mine.

"Yeah. But that was a strong one." He glances at his watch.

I just get tuned in again to the pastor's message when another one comes. I grab my husband's hand and put it on my firm stomach. "Another one . . . already," I whisper.

Wide eyed, he rips off his watch and starts pushing buttons. "I'd better start timing them." On the back of the bulletin he scrawls a crude chart.

Three minutes later, another one comes. Two and a half minutes later, another. Then, five minutes later. Then two. Then three and a half. I have been having the contractions off and on for several months. But not like this. Each one, so steady and strong. Could this be it?

After the service, a small group gathers around us. When the word got out that we had been timing contractions instead of taking notes, the excitement began to buzz through our small congregation.

"I'll bet you'll be taking a trip to the hospital tonight," someone comments. "Let us know as soon as that baby's born."

When the last of the congregation has filtered through the front door, my husband helps me up from my seat. He leads me out the side door and down the long cement ramp to the parking lot, holding in one hand my clammy hand, and clutching in the other his watch.

Back at home.

Should we try to ignore the contractions, or call the doctor?

We both are starving. But I know I shouldn't eat. As we learned in childbirth class, once you're in labor, no eating solid foods. Water, clear juices, jello, broth—Yes. Granola, cinnamon-raisin bagels, nachos, pizza—No way.

But *he* can eat. He needs to eat. If this *is* the real thing, he will need every calorie to help him call out numbers while I breathe. Still, hungry as he is, he prowls the house instead of eating.

A couple of hours pass. I lie on the couch on my side, and he sits clear across the room with his watch. We both pretend to watch TV; we even stare at the commercials as if we're enthralled.

Suddenly a strong contraction grips my stomach. He starts the stopwatch and pencils the time on a Post-it pad. "I think you should call the doctor and just see what he says."

"I do too. It can't hurt," I say. He gets up from his chair and brings me the phone, already dialed.

"Hi, Doctor. This is Julie Martin. I've been having pretty strong contractions all day, and they don't seem to be getting any easier. Pardon? . . . Uh huh. Yes. About two minutes apart. No. Not due for two more weeks. Okay. We'll give you a call."

"Well?" my husband asks, hanging up the phone.

"He says to give it till midnight, and if they're still getting stronger, come on in. Oh, I really want to be sure this is it before we go to the hospital. I don't want to be sent home."

"You also don't want to have the baby in the car," he quickly responds.

"You're right, dear," I say wryly. "Hey, let's go for a walk. I read that if it's false labor, walking will slow the

[91]

contractions down. But if it's real labor, it'll speed them up."

It's 11:00 P.M. We put on our tennis shoes, turn on the front porch light, and start briskly walking down the street of our dark neighborhood. Just a few houses down, a contraction comes. I stop and bend down, resting my hands on my thighs.

"Is this it?" he asks.

"I don't know," I answer, looking at the asphalt street.

Every block or so, another one comes, stronger than the one before.

"I think this is it," I say with a cramped voice.

Then, they quit coming. We walk, and I wait for that hot tightness, but it doesn't come. "I don't think this is for real, honey. They're going away."

But just then, another one grips me. "Is this it?" he asks.

"I don't know. All I know is that it hurts!"

He puts his arm around my shoulder. "Come on, let's get home."

The quiet neighborhood whispers that it is almost midnight. We walk silently up our short driveway, and then another contraction hits me hard. As if it were bright noon, I blurt, "Sweetheart, this may be it!"

The bag is packed, complete with chewing gum, a racquetball to help relieve back labor, and vaseline for chapped lips from breathing through the mouth. Everything is set except for one: my husband's stomach. He's hungry. In all his anxiousness, he still hasn't eaten.

On our way to the hospital, we stop at an all-night cafe for a submarine sandwich. He orders a club special, hold the onions, while I sit at the booth and wait.

Holding his foot-long sandwich like a prize, he joins me at our booth and quickly unwraps the food. It smells tantalizingly delicious, as all forbidden fruit so cruelly does. But I don't dare take even so much as a bite. Not if I really am in labor.

While I sit and he eats, we talk. Talk about who to call when the baby is born, and how we'd better decide on a boy's name, and how awful it would be to get sent home.

We talk, and I think how strange it is—it must be part of Eve's curse—that I will be doing all the work, yet he is the one who gets to eat.

We are here.

The hospital is nine stories of small rooms full of people. Some healing, some dying, and some, like me, about to give birth.

Once inside, we are met by a smile at the front desk. There is no question as to why we have come.

i have wondered what it's like to sit in the wheelchair
  let the nurse wheel me down the hall to the labor room
    wheel me down the hall
and now it's really happening
  to me

i have wondered what it's like to be wheeled down the hall
  on the fresh polished floor
  clean walls on both sides, hospital smell thick in the air
  hospital smell in the air

i have wondered what it's like to sign the admittance form
  sign my name on the thin line at the bottom of the page
    sign my name on the line

i have wondered what it's like to know that within a day
  i'd give my baby birth
  survive delivery and be holding my baby
    holding my baby
and now it's really going to happen to me
  to me
and now it's really happening to me

3:00 A.M.

The nurse comes in to tell us that I'm really in labor; and although it's slow, we're here to stay. After she leaves, my husband squeezes my hand, then moves slowly to the window to look outside at the city's lights. He is quiet. And I know what he's thinking. It's here, this moment. Our hearts are overripe with anticipation, but soon the dream—the child—will be known.

And with the baby, another new life will be born—our new life as parents. Our new life as a union inseparably bound to a small person, vulnerable, needy, dependent.

We will have to be givers, accepters, no-strings-attached lovers. Our child will need his being embraced as much as he will ever need nourishment or warmth.

Lying on my side on the crisp white sheet, I watch my husband as he looks out the window. He stares blankly through the night, hand stroking his stubbly chin. A father is about to be born.

It's still black morning.

I'm lying in bed in a hospital gown. The IV drips into
my needled hand. The fetal monitor wraps itself around
my stomach like a bow around a package. A styrofoam
cup full of ice chips rests on the tray at my right. My
husband dozes in the recliner by the window. And that
clock on the wall—the hands are standing still.

Time continues to crawl until noon, when labor picks
up and I forget all about the clock. All I can think about is
the pain—Lamaze's number one no-no.

"Help me with my breathing," I say gruffly.

My husband gets up from the chair and stands at the
side of the bed.

"Three," he calls out.

I take my three quick breaths and listen for the next
number.

"Five."

"That's too long. I'll hyperventilate," I complain.

He calls out, "Two."

The nurse stops in every half hour or so. She checks
for dilation, takes my temperature, brings me more ice
chips. This kindred stranger in white cares about me and
my baby. And even though she is being paid for her
kindness, I get the feeling that if she had to, she would do
it for free.

"How are we doing?" she asks my husband. I'm
concentrating too hard to answer.

"She's hurtin'."

"Let's check and see how she's progressing," the
nurse says. And then: "She's at six centimeters. It
shouldn't be long."

I need him with me, here in the room. He has gone to the lobby to give our parents the progress report when a contraction comes that makes the room shrink and the plaid wallpaper blur. I can't think about breathing or about that beach on Maui. All I can think about is how afraid I am, how badly I need him with me here in the room.

Again, time freezes.

Nine hours pass in what seems like either nine minutes or a week—I can't tell which.

I am there, yet not. My husband and the nurse are talking. The sound of their voices annoys me, yet I do not even hear them. Working hard yet mindlessly, I have forgotten why I'm here.

I am trying just to endure each minute.
Endure.

Have to have to push. Never had to do anything in my life. Oh, have to push, as bad as I have to here it comes, "Come on, come on, Come on," the three of them yell. "Good one! We can see the baby's head." *I am having a baby, that's right, that's, oh, here comes another . . . push . . . bone squeezing through bone. How will the head ever get through? How will it?* "One more and we'll have it." *Give it everything you've . . . oh, push.* Time stands . . . lost, lost in frozen time till "That's it! That's it!" *The head. Out. Suction sounds. Clearing the baby's nose and throat. But still have to push. One more. I will die if I can't . . . push . . . hot liquid, hot. Hot. And soft flesh sliding . . . there's the baby. The baby.* Doctor says, "What have we got?" *Eyes hot, can't see quite. Burning. It's a girl, a baby girl. Big surprise. Beautiful. Beautiful. Erica Lynn. Puts her hot head on my stomach. Stroking the wet flesh. Please cry. I want to hear you cry. A cry, scratchy, lusty, beautiful. Long and hard.* Then she looks up at me and stills. Looks up at me and stills.

A woman giving birth to a child has pain because her time has come; but when her baby is born she forgets the anguish because of her joy that a child is born into the world.

John 16:21

Visiting hours bring friends and family to see the new baby—oh yes, and to see me too.

I am still tired and weak. But I will gladly accept any excuse to get out of that bed, walk down the hall, and gaze at her through the glass window.

I show my visitors to the nursery. "Baby Martin. Girl," reads the sticker on her clear plastic bassinet. There she is. I point her out.

She's asleep. Her lips are pursed to form a gentle "O." It's hard work, being born.

We stand there for a while: I in my slippers and robe; they in their street clothes. They tell me she is beautiful. I say thank you and yes, isn't she. But never before have I known words to be so inadequate.

She is one of about twenty swaddled babies in the nursery today. But she is the only one I see.

It's time to go home, the three of us. I am sitting on the bed waiting for the nurse to bring the discharge papers. My husband is loading the car, and my mom, who has come to help us with the baby, sits glowing in the chair by my bed.

"Mrs. Martin?" a nurse calls from behind the curtain.

"Yes, come in."

Pulling the curtain back with a *swoosh,* she answers, "I've got the wheelchair. Your doctor gave the okay for you to go home. As soon as you're ready, I'll get your baby."

"Okay, great. I think I'm ready."

Just then, my husband walks in, empty-armed. "Hi. Can we go?"

"Yeah, honey, here's my wheelchair. The nurse went to get the baby."

He walks around the bed to help ease me into the wheelchair. The curtain sways. A hand appears and draws the curtain toward the wall. In the other arm, the nurse cradles the baby. Her eyes are open. She is bundled tight. The nurse places her in my arms. "Are we ready?" she says.

"Yes." My husband and I answer together.

We ride down the corridor like we're in a parade. There are no horses, clowns, or marching bands. But there is a dance in the air, a joy that balloons in the hallway and revels in our hearts. People stop to admire her as we ride by. They shower us with their smiles and comments like confetti. These strangers lining the sides of the path celebrate with us the new life in my arms.

The wheelchair rolls across the electronic mat, and instantly, briskly opens the hospital's front double doors. The spring wind whips in from outside. I hold the baby a little closer and pull the receiving blanket up to cover her paper-thin ears.

"It's cold," I tell her. "Daddy's going to get the car and then we'll take you home."

My husband pulls up the car as cautiously as if the curb were a bassinet. He hops out of the front seat and carefully takes her from my arms, one hand under her wobbly head, the other under her thickly diapered bottom. The car seat is fastened in, facing backwards, exactly as we had been told to do it.

"Are you sure this is how it's supposed to be buckled?" I ask, looking over his shoulder as he straps the baby in.

"Yeah. This is how they told us in class, remember?"

"That's right." It's our baby we're talking about. Every jot and tittle of baby-care law must be heeded.

He buckles up, starts the car, and looks over his shoulder to see how we are. "Are you ready?"

Belted tight into the back seat, I lean over as far as I can to snatch another close look at her. Despite our miserable inexperience, she sleeps. She is wrapped like a mummy, bottom lip protruding and shiny with drool. "Yeah. But go slow."

So he drives and I watch. I police every car within fifty feet. After all, every car is a potential accident. And why don't they all just pull over? Don't they know we have a newborn in the car?

Finally, we turn the last corner home. And as we approach our house, we see the pink banner hung across our garage door: IT'S A GIRL!

you've only been here a few hours
but already you have changed this place
you have filled the empty room in this house
        in our hearts
already you have made this house
a home

She's all ours.

What do we do?

In the hospital, the nurses took care of her. They checked her, changed her, soothed her. Every four hours they brought her to me so I could feed her, but when she was through they wheeled her away, back to the nurses with name tags and clean hands.

But now she's all ours.

What if she starts crying and won't stop? How will I know if she gets sick? She's so floppy, how will I ever be able to bathe her? What if she stops breathing? What if she's cold and doesn't know how to tell us?

What do we do? She's all ours.

*. . . He gathers the lambs in his arms
and carries them close to his heart;
he gently leads those that have young.*
                    Isaiah 40:11

Asleep, until your delicate cry cracks open an eyelid of the night. It's feeding time, for both of us. I stroke your warm head, nurse your drowsy body. And you, tiny hand on my breast, you nourish my soul. Although day is dawning somewhere across the globe, to me the whole world is you and me, the dim lamp in the corner, and the moon.

The days and nights are all the same. I sleep when she sleeps, light or dark. And when she's awake during the day, I talk to her, feed her, change her, bathe her, or sing songs to lull her back to sleep.

It's as though I'm existing only to keep her alive.

I had always imagined we would spend our first few weeks together outside; she would nap in her shaded playpen while I gardened or read in the sun. But I'm afraid it'll be awhile before I pick up a spade. They tell me it'll change. "Soon, she'll put herself on a schedule and you'll be able to plan your day around it," I have heard.

But for now I am tired. And I don't care if I never read another novel or pull another weed.

She was born old.

Red and wrinkled, like a bruised plum. Toothless,
bony, bald. Her thin skin clung to her frail frame like
cellophane to a plate of bones, showing the color of her
veins, the sections of her skull. And her vision, clouded as
with the film of a cataract. In the beginning she slept the
days away, demanding only food and warmth and
comfort—as if she were on her death bed.

Yet within her, life is thriving. Each day her body
plumps and whitens. Each day her eyes brighten; the
clouds are lifting. Each day her personality awakens; she
smiles.

An anomaly, it is. The newly born in an elderly body.
Growing every day more young.

It's an ordinary morning. I have just given her a bath in her padded, plastic tub. Her head smells like pink sunshine, and her dark hair curls damply at the dough-white nape of her neck. I place her on her back in the crib and reach for a diaper. When my cold hand touches her satiny skin, she squirms and coos, and, with great effort, rolls over onto her tummy. I pat the small, irresistible bottom as any mother would.

"Let's turn you over so Mommy can get a diaper on you." She smiles and coos, grabbing at my dangling hair.

After barraging me with friendly kicks and twists to avoid the diaper, she catches the light streaming in through the cracks of her mini-blinds, stops, and stares. Now's my chance. With one hand, I grab her plump ankles and lift her legs off the crib sheet. Then I slip the diaper underneath her, and quickly secure the tabs.

"There, all done, honey."

My voice arouses her from her gaze. She looks into my face, curling her cherry-red lips to make sweet vowel sounds.

Smiling, I grab her feet and pump her chubby legs, slowly at first, and then increasingly faster as I make the sounds of a choo-choo train. "Choo! Choo! Choo! Choo!"

Her eyes brighten. Her mouth opens wide. And then, I hear the sound I will never forget. For the first time, this three-and-a-half-month-old baby girl laughs. Not just a chuckle—a belly laugh. She does it again and again. The faster I "choo" her legs, the harder she laughs. And I, wet-eyed, am hysterical.

We are communicating.

She understands the meaning of silly.

This new laughter is bubbles to my ears and a rippling brook in my soul.

It's morning.

Holding her in my arms I open the front door. The cool air bathes her face. Her eyes widen, eyebrows rise. She draws a quick breath. A tiny leg begins to kick against my thigh.

She lunges to greet it, whatever it is she sees that makes her feel so very alive.

The sun. The fresh, silent sound in the air. The *swoosh* of a car driving swiftly past.

It's morning.

Her morning.

She greets it well.

I watch her from across the room. She crawls along and spots some treasure in the corner. With Olympic concentration, she traps it between two clumsy pincers and puts it in her mouth. It could be a penny or a cockroach, for all I know. So I bound toward her and calmly call her name. Before I reach her, she opens wide her mouth to show me the gem. A Cheerio. Mushy, but still intact.

Cheerios. They're everywhere.

Soggy and shrunken on the walker's plastic tray. Smashed in the car seat, in the washer, between pages in books. Sopped Cheerio pieces, dangling from the seat of the high chair. Cheerio powder trailed along the kitchen floor.

They are a kind of O-shaped Easter egg, hidden away in every nook and cranny, waiting for a finder who is ready for a snack.

Give her a handful in the kitchen, and the next day they're all over the house.

She hunts them. Who hides them?

They breed at night and wander. They must.

She's especially tired today, and will need help going down for her nap. With one hand I drag the rocking chair from the corner of the room, leaving tracks in the soft gray carpet. When I sit down on its cold seat, the old wooden rocker creaks. Her eyes widen for a moment. But as I begin to rock, as the creaks become hypnotically rhythmic, her eyelids start to droop. With each forward motion they sag further, and then open again when I push off from the carpet with the balls of my feet. It's as if she's conducting the chair with her eyes.

Soon she's asleep. The need is taken care of, the soothing done. I watch the tiny chest that swells with each sleeping breath. The dark, wispy hair that forms a gyre at her crown. The fingers, a row of small sausages, resting against my shoulder.

Yes, she's asleep. I can put her down now, I know.

But I will go on rocking for a while.

The front door swings wide open and bumps the wall with a clunk as we drag the tree into the house. Once we're inside, I run to pick up the baby.

"See the Christmas tree?" I say, pointing to the fresh Douglas fir. Wearing her red-and-white sleeper, her brow crinkled, this nine-month-old girl studies the tree. Her daddy closes the front door and drags the tree across the living room to its spot against the wall. I set her down. She peers around my legs, watching his every move.

Finally, the tree is standing. She takes one last long look, and then curiosity propels her to touch it. So she crawls over to the tree, slowly, stopping to poke at the loose pine needles that clutter the floor. When she finally gets to the tree, she reaches out to touch its green needles. But she finds their prickly tips uninviting, and, eyes still glued, scoots away from the tree.

I put on the Christmas music and light the candles; her daddy brings in the boxes of ornaments and lights.

"Christmas candles, honey. They're pretty," I tell her. She looks up at me with delight. She knows by my voice that "pretty" is good.

We string the lights around the tree, hang the ornaments on its full branches. And she watches, eyes darting from candles to tree to twinkling lights to stereo speaker when the music tickles her ears.

Before we finish the decorating, she gives a big yawn and lays her head down on the carpet. Hearing her silent request for bed, her daddy scoops her up and takes her to her crib.

Her room is dark. But with her, into her dreams, she carries images of the room she left, alive with flickering light.

erica it's Christmas
and what can that mean to you
   but the bright lights on the tree
   the packages, shimmering with gold ribbons and
      bows
   the green wreath on the door
   and the candles that make the walls dance
      with their shadows

someday you will know the real Christmas
   if you see bright love in our lives
   pure devotion to God, glistening gold
   commitment nailed on the door of our hearts
   and the word of the Son that will make your heart
      dance with its light
then you will know that He has come
and that He has come to make you whole

It's impish, I know.

I usually don't even risk disturbing her while she's napping. But I can't help wondering how she wakes, what it is she first sees, and what she would think of finding me there, in her room, without her calling me in. If I could just sneak into her room right before she was due to wake up, and wait there, maybe I could see.

I turn the cool brass knob of her door slowly, silently, crack open the door, and peer in. Cheek smashed against the drooly sheet, she's still sound asleep. The back of her careless head is still. In fact, all of her is still, except her young back, which softly swells with each breath.

I slip through the door and close it quietly behind me.

She doesn't move.

The artful part will be getting from the door to the floor by the crib—the wood floor crackles and creaks with each step. Three big steps and I'll be there. I lift a foot and step down. The floor squeals.

But she doesn't move.

I lift the other foot and take a step. A loud pop from the floor.

She draws a deep breath and shifts her head.

Just one more step and I'll have it.

As I set my foot down for the last time, the floor is silent. I made it. I lie down parallel to the crib with my head at her feet, so I can have a clear view of her face when she wakes. Her breathing is again steady and slow. I may be here a while.

Lying on my back, I scan the room. Balloon print wallpaper. Afternoon sunlight seeping through mini-blind cracks. Stacks of diapers on the shelf. A beach ball in the corner. Yes, I've seen them all before. But never from the eyes of the baby who knows them as the dependable world she leaves and returns to from sleep.

Rustling sheets rouse me. She draws her knees up under her body and lets an arm fly. One tiny finger pokes through the slats in a slump.

She is still again.

Then suddenly, the moment I've been waiting for. She lifts her head, and, yawning big, looks around. She doesn't see me, but continues to scan the room, her head twitching like a sparrow perched on a branch.

After getting her bearings, she makes her move. A tiny hand reaches for the closest slat and pulls her toward the railing. Then, hand over hand, she pulls herself up to stand against the guard rail. She still doesn't see me, even from her panoramic view of the room; and it isn't long before she lets out her somebody-come-get-me call.

"Hi, honey," I call from the floor.

She freezes, then, wide eyed, looks down at me and smiles, pounding the guard rail with a flat palm.

"You had a big nap. Are you all rested?" I say to her, getting up from my spot on the floor.

As I bend to pick her up, she reaches both arms up to me.

"Hi. Mommy missed you."

We walk to the window and open the blinds. We stop to talk to the balloons on the walls. I turn the warm brass knob of her door quickly. And, together, we leave the room.

It's not a sense of wonder that propels you, celebrating, through your world. Wonder is only known by the grown-up mind, which doesn't expect life to be interesting, wonderful, beautiful, and so is surprised when it finds itself staring beauty in the face.

No, you know nothing about wonder. That the moon comes out at night to shine its pale light, that water stirs when you glide a hand through it, that banana squishes through your fingers when you squeeze—these discoveries do not amaze you. They only confirm what you, in your barefoot heart, already know as truth.

Teaching you to be like Jesus is my most important goal as a mother. But the more I try, the more I question who teaches whom. You seem to be so much like Him, without even having to try.

Your conscience is cloudless, swaddled in purity, as you crawl through your days.

You forgive and forget before the tears ever dry on your face.

You never doubt love.

I want to be like you, learn from you, love like you, my child.

Therefore, whoever humbles himself like this child is the greatest in the kingdom of heaven.
Matthew 18:4

You are our firstborn child.

You will always be our oldest, the one who broke us in.

We will tell you about the brother or sister you would have had when you are old enough to understand, in your own, pure nursery-school way, death and loss and the bigness of God's plan.

Daddy and I will always carry a small ache in our hearts for the baby that came and died before you. And you might too; because it hurts to love.

But please, let yourself wonder if the baby was a brother or a sister, if he was blue-eyed or brown, if he would have been proud of you. And know that you will have answers some day. Your older brother or sister lives in heaven with Jesus. And some day you will meet.

Filled with morning light, the church is alive. We have just finished singing the hymn. The last chord hangs in the air, rich as worship, while we reach to return our hymnals to the wooden rack on the back of the pew. Our pastor walks down the platform stairs and stands at the front. "Would those who are dedicating their children please come on up?"

I side-step my way out of the pew and wait for my husband and the baby, who sleeps in his arms, and together we walk to the front of the church to join a whole row of parents and their young children.

The pastor reads Scripture telling what a blessing children are, what a miracle, what a gift. He reminds us that we don't own them, that they have been loaned to us by God to love and teach and model His love.

The pastor then turns toward us, smiles warmly, and addresses the congregation. "This is little Erica. Alan, would you lead us in prayer for Erica's life?"

My husband prays for her. He asks that she will be sensitive to God and early come to know Him. He prays for us. That we will keep a loose grasp on her life and show His love by our lives.

She's asleep. And doesn't hear a word. But I pray that she will see what was said this warm morning. I pray that she will see.

we are your everything
when your daddy cut the cord it was
   only the beginning of dependency
    for from our hearts you will take all you need
and the best we can give you is Jesus
   the best we can show you is His love so that one
      day
all you need will come from His heart and
He will be your everything

HANNAH'S SONG

(see 1 Samuel 1:21–28)

Hannah, even before Samuel was born he was God's
You had vowed that if God would
*   just give you a son*
You would give him back

He was just a chubby toddler when you sent him
*   away,*
*   just learning to wonder why*
Did he ask you why he had to go
Why you couldn't stay with him there
Did his sweet voice and liquid eyes
*   make you want to change your mind*

You sent him like you promised
And visited him once a year
*   holding in your arms the new robe*
*   you had made with your hands*
Every stitch was a prayer
*   every thread a cord of commitment*
In these costly gifts you clothed your son
You must have left him each year with a singing
*   heart*
Because you had seen that God was still hearing you
That Samuel was learning to know God's voice when
*   He called*
*   and that with a young trust he answered*
*   "Here I am"*

When Samuel was old enough to leave her, Hannah took him to Shiloh and with this prayer dedicated her son to the Lord.

My heart rejoices in the LORD;
  in the LORD my horn is lifted high.
My mouth boasts over my enemies,
  for I delight in your deliverance.

There is no one holy like the LORD;
  there is no one besides you;
  there is no Rock like our God.

The LORD brings death and makes alive;
  he brings down to the grave and raises up.
The LORD sends poverty and wealth;
  he humbles and he exalts.
He raises the poor from the dust
  and lifts the needy from the ash heap;
he seats them with princes
  and has them inherit a throne of honor.
For the foundations of the earth are the LORD's;
  upon them he has set the world.

1 Samuel 2:1, 2, 6–8